THE CHRISTMAS HELPER

Tips and Inspiration for a Festive and Merry Holiday Season

LIA MANEA

DEDICATION

I dedicate this book to all those who enjoy a
healthy dose of anticipation before Christmas, hum
"Jingle Bells" throughout December and can't wait
for those magical moments with friends and family
around the Christmas tree.
I also dedicate this book to my amazing son, to
my wonderful husband, to my "Christmas spirit"
enthusiast sister, to my parents and to all my family.
I love you all and I am really grateful for having you
in my life.

Contents

HOW TO USE THIS BOOK

Each chapter can be read as a stand-alone resource so feel free to jump around to find whatever you need, as you need them. For instance, if you feel like reading some good holiday jokes, go ahead and skip to Chapter 11 right now.

I also intended this to be timeless, so you can flip through it each holiday season, make necessary notes and updates in the tables or gift some copies to your closest friends!

Enjoy!

1 INTRODUCTION

Gifts of time and love are surely the basic ingredients of a truly merry Christmas

- PEG BRACKEN, American Author

The true magic of Christmas comes from something intangible: a mix of anticipation, childhood memories, the smell of freshly baked goodies, the chatter of family members, the joy in the children's eyes when they unwrap presents and from feeling grateful and happy.

The secret of a blissful Christmas lies not in how much money you spend, but in how you spend your time and how much you care about the people in your life.

From a more practical point of view, the secret of a perfect Christmas lies also in **careful planning and organizing**. Forward preparations can take care of some chores that might otherwise keep you from the more whimsical activities – such as staring at the Christmas tree or sipping mulled wine curled up on the sofa. Sure, a combination of the two works just as fine.

The **holiday planners, lists and trackers** in Chapter 2 will keep you on top of things.

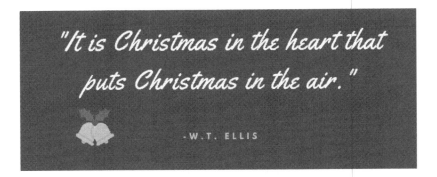

"It is Christmas in the heart that puts Christmas in the air."

-W.T. ELLIS

Truth be told, some of the more tangible things related to Christmas can add just as much joy and magic as the previously mentioned intangible ones. I'm thinking of Christmas lights, themed decorations, winter scene puzzles, Santa figurines, elf outfits, mistletoe, Christmas tunes and movies and all those little things that add to the holiday atmosphere.

You'll find some **fun games** and some **festive jokes** in Chapters 8 and 11 to keep you entertained while you drink that hot cocoa.

This book is filled with **tips and inspiration** to help you create a blissful celebration this year, one that will be remembered for years and years to come until it finally becomes the stuff of legends. I might be exaggerating a tad, but you will find stellar advice about choosing thoughtful gifts, a couple mouth-watering recipes, priceless templates for lists and trackers, project ideas to make with the kids, a timeless classic Christmas story, suggestions of themed books and movies to read and watch this wonderful time of year, home décor advice plus a few pointers for how to help the environment.

Enjoy the holidays and be merry!

2 PLANNING AND ANTICIPATION

**"*City sidewalks*
Busy sidewalks,
Dressed in holiday style
In the air
There's a feeling
Of Christmas..."**

- SILVER BELLS

Planning ahead and doing a bit of forward thinking can help you enjoy the actual Christmas events and activities, rather than rushing to do everything last minute.

This chapter will give you some **tips and tools** so keep things organized.

COME NOVEMBER

It's time to draft a Christmas budget and to start a list of Christmas ideas to keep at hand (on your smartphone, your PC or on a nice piece of paper). For those who like to be even more organized, a **Christmas Gifts Tracker**, a **Christmas Card Mailing List,** a **Holiday Bucket List,** an **Online Order Tracker,** a **December Calendar Planner** and a **Christmas Parties and Events Planner** could get in handy. You'll find them listed at the end of this chapter.

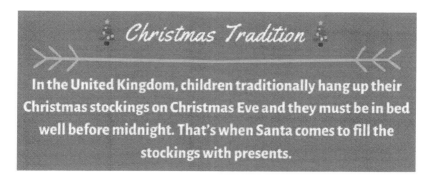

Christmas Tradition

In the United Kingdom, children traditionally hang up their Christmas stockings on Christmas Eve and they must be in bed well before midnight. That's when Santa comes to fill the stockings with presents.

It's easy to get caught up in the general holiday spirit and end up overspending.

Should you plan to go to a Christmas show, musical, ballet or theatre, take care of the bookings several months ahead.

This is my mantra and you should know that it's never too early to start thinking about Christmas shopping. I know this is extreme, but one time I found an extraordinary cute Santa themed gift for a niece a month after Christmas so I got it anyways and offered it the next year. Of course, she loved it and for me it was worth the wait.

Begin by filling in the **Christmas Gift Tracker** with the list of people you wish to buy presents for and don't forget to start scribbling down ideas in early November (at the latest). Mark any presents that will have to be sent by mail so that you may ensure there is enough time for delivery.

Start working on your **Christmas Card Mailing List** in mid-November and check that addresses are all up to date.

Now it's also the time to buy an Advent calendar if you like to count down the days towards Christmas. Children love that, it's a great way to build anticipation. By the beginning of December, you can buy them at discounted prices. Another idea is to make one yourself, or with the help of the children.

If you're hosting a Christmas Party, make sure to get your party invites out early so that people have time to RSVP.

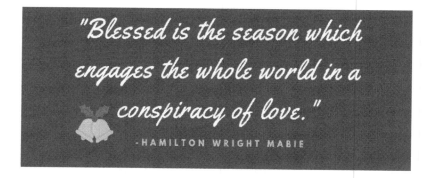

"Blessed is the season which engages the whole world in a conspiracy of love."
-HAMILTON WRIGHT MABIE

For the gifts that you order online, don't forget to take into account an extra time buffer in the event you have to send something back.

Don't forget that December is a busy month for hairdressers and beauty salons so make your appointments early.

COME DECEMBER

This is the perfect time to start decorating your home. Welcome the festive season with a wreath on your front door and the outdoor Christmas lights. More on Christmas home décor in Chapter 3.

You should plan in advance your outfits for the holiday parties and events. Perhaps you can wear the same outfit more than once for different party crowds – that would help both your budget and the environment. A mere change of accessories for the same outfit can work wonders.

Start mailing the **Christmas cards** in the first week of December and in mid-December for the local ones.

Don't forget to think of the **holiday menu** and grocery list, some recipes need fancy ingredients and now's the time to do some shopping before the Christmas Craze.

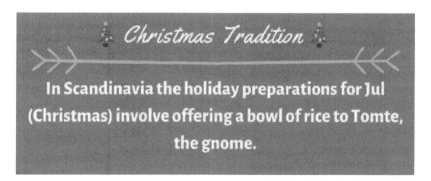

Christmas Tradition

In Scandinavia the holiday preparations for Jul (Christmas) involve offering a bowl of rice to Tomte, the gnome.

Now's also the time to make sure you have all the **wrapping** paper you need for your gifts. It's best to wrap the presents as soon as possible, to avoid any last-minute wrapping sessions. A poor wrapping paper or a plastic bag can surely undermine what would otherwise be a very inspired and beautiful gift.

Don't forget the labels, you don't want the gifts to get mixed!

Avoid the busiest times at the shops — mornings and weekdays are best for dodging the crowds. Always have the budget in mind and the list of gift ideas at hand. There is such a variety of things on offer at Christmas time that it's easy to become overwhelmed or overexcited and thus end up **overspending**.

Do your budget a favor and keep an eye out for 'three for two' and 'buy one get one free' type of offers.

Make sure you have **some stand-by presents** — bottle of wine, chocolates, festive-themed items — on hand. You might go to some unexpected events or some new guests could be announced for some parties or family reunions.

CHRISTMAS TREE

You must figure out when it's the best time to put the Christmas tree up. Traditionally, trees were put up on Christmas Eve, but nowadays things got really complicated...or quite the contrary.

A plastic Christmas tree can be put up and decorated at the very beginning of December, it will not dry out. But for a real tree you will need to consider how long it will stay fresh and make sure you water it regularly. Too many people have been left with piles of dry needles by Christmas Day. Make sure the tree is sustainably sourced and that it has been planted for this very purpose.

I have a very beautiful ex-Christmas tree that I planted in my front yard 7 years ago. So, consider replanting the tree somewhere if you have this choice.

If you can brave the crowds and you have time to spare, it can be worth hitting the shops on Christmas Eve to grab a few bargains as many of them already begin discounting items.

"Christmas waves a magic wand over this world, and behold, everything is softer and more beautiful."

-NORMAN VINCENT PEALE

THE WEEK BEFORE CHRISTMAS

Take care of any last-minute shopping, check the cupboard and double check the **Christmas Gifts Tracker**. Shop for your last items of fresh produce such as milk, bread and fruit and vegetables. Make sure you don't have to interrupt the festive celebrations with an emergency supermarket run.

Get out some Christmas biscuits, sweets and treats to create a festive display just in case you have any unexpected visitors.

CHRISTMAS CARD MAILING LIST

Take 5 minutes to think of some people that you did not see for a long time, they live far away and you will not get to see them this holiday season. Why not spread some festive cheer far and wide by sending them handwritten Christmas cards?

I'm sure you have some dear friends or relatives that would

really appreciate receiving a season's greeting from you.

Buy more cards than there are names on your list, just in case you've forgotten anyone. They'll be just as good for next year, should you not need them.

Just to get your inspiration going, check out these **holiday cards** from long ago.

STAR, YOU CAN LEAD
ME ALL THE WAY
THRO DARKEST NIGHT
AND BRIGHTEST DAY

TO ALL THIS
CANDLE LIGHT
IS BEAMING
WITH CHRISTMAS
JOY IN ALL ITS
GLEAMING

I'M ALWAYS SAFE
WHEN MY GOOD STAR
GUIDES ME AT HOME
OR WAYWARD FAR

HERE IS A BRANCH
OF BARBERRY
SENT IN GOOD OLD
FASHIONED STYLE
MAY IT BRING A
CHRISTMAS MERRY
AND EVERYTHING
ELSE WORTH WHILE

THE CHRISTMAS CANDLE
SHEDS ITS LIGHT
AND BRINGS GOOD CHEER
ON CHRISTMAS NIGHT

THESE LITTLE BIRDS SO
LIGHT AND FREE
BRING CHRISTMAS JOY
FOR YOU AND ME.

MAY YULETIDE
CHEER
BE YOURS THIS
YEAR

RING MERRY BELLS
AND SCATTER
WIDE
THE HAPPINESS
OF CHRISTMAS
TIDE

HERE'S A MERRY
CHRISTMAS TO YOU
MAY IT LAST THE
WHOLE YEAR THROUGH

EPIC LISTS AND TRACKERS

And last but not least, behold the **epic lists and trackers** that will help you get organized for the holidays.

As a gift, I am making the **Templates** available for all the readers of this book in printable format as well. Just send an email to lia.manea.perfectgift@gmail.com and you'll receive the download link.

Or, you could type the link in your browser:
https://storyoriginapp.com/giveaways/688e1c24-c90e-11ea-aed1-cb3f13679c84

All you have to do is print your favorite ones each year and use the templates over and over again. Enjoy!

Holiday Bucket List

CREATE	ENJOY	LIVE
To Make, Bake or Shake	At Home Read, Do, Watch	Out and About

December

SUNDAY	MONDAY	TUESDAY	WEDNESDAY	THURSDAY	FRIDAY	SATURDAY

Santa's List

Who?

Gift Ideas

Christmas Gifts Tracker

Who?

Gift

Purchased ☐

Budget

Store

Wrapped ☐

Who?

Gift

Purchased ☐

Budget

Store

Wrapped ☐

Who?

Gift

Purchased ☐

Budget

Store

Wrapped ☐

Christmas Card Mailing List

Name
Address
Sent date

Name
Address
Sent date

Name
Address
Sent date

Name
Address
Sent date

Name
Address
Sent date

Online Order Tracker

Item	Online Shop	Date ordered	Notes	Received
				☐
				☐
				☐
				☐
				☐
				☐
				☐
				☐
				☐
				☐
				☐
				☐
				☐
				☐
				☐
				☐
				☐
				☐

Christmas Parties and Events Planner

Date	Event	Time	Notes

3 DECK THE HALLS: HOME DÉCOR TIPS

"Oh, the weather outside is frightful,
But the fire is so delightful,
And since we've no place to go,
Let it snow, let it snow, let it snow."

\-   LET IT SNOW

Lots of people like to get their Christmas decorations up at the start of December. I'm definitely one of those people.

Give in to your inner Elf and take inspiration from this chapter to add a touch of festivity to every corner of your home.

Decorating the house is a fun activity, preferably done with friends or family members. Bake (or buy) some fresh cookies, put on a jolly Christmas playlist and fill the house with festive smells and sounds.

If you'd like to add a more designed look to your Christmas décor, try picking a **color scheme** before beginning to decorate.

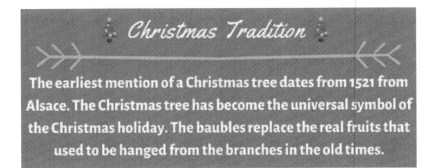

Christmas Tradition

The earliest mention of a Christmas tree dates from 1521 from Alsace. The Christmas tree has become the universal symbol of the Christmas holiday. The baubles replace the real fruits that used to be hanged from the branches in the old times.

WARM AND COZY COLOR SCHEME

This fits best with a rustic vibe, solid wood furniture and a more classic interior design. A *red and green traditional look* will get everyone in the Christmas mood. Accessories from natural materials in warm colors, such as pine cones, cotton runners and tartan dinnerware will complement the look.

WHITE MAGIC COLOR SCHEME

Snow and ice is always a popular and elegant look and it's usually a good fit with modern interiors. Warm it up with touches of gold and bronze – in the Christmas tree, napkin rings, place mats and other decorations.

BOLD GOLDS

A strong, gold color scheme creates a glamorous look and the wow factor is guaranteed. Make sure the Christmas lights are all warm white, otherwise the contrast will be unpleasant. Add to the warm vibes with gold jingle bells, metallic gold porcelain and large baubles.

THE RED LINE

No matter what color scheme or look you choose, be coherent by keeping the same general style throughout the house. In interior design this is called the principle of the red line. Having a rustic, warm look in the hallway followed by a white magic color scheme in the Livingroom is not a good idea.

A balanced environment gives a sense of well-being and harmony.

> *"Like snowflakes, my Christmas memories gather and dance - each beautiful, unique, and gone too soon."*
> -DEBORAH WHIPP

FESTIVE CENTERPIECE

This is where you can get really creative and you can find lots of ideas on the Internet on places such as Pinterest or just by googling. Just make sure it's in line with the chosen decorative scheme of your house.

CHRISTMAS CARDS DISPLAY

A cute and colorful idea is to display the Christmas cards received over the years somewhere in your living room, maybe near the tree or the sitting area. The easiest method is to string some ribbon or thin tinsel across the corner of a room or along a mantelpiece or some other convenient place. Just look around the room and you'll surely find the perfect location. Attach the cards with small clothes pegs.

This display gives a cozy vibe and you can be constantly reminded of all the good wishes and the season's greetings sheltered in the Christmas cards.

OUTDOOR MAGIC

Drape outdoor fairy lights around small potted trees or your garden plants to create a magical pathway to your front door.

Wrap everything up with a bunch of mistletoe tied with ribbon and hung from a doorway. The perfect place to stop for a traditional festive kiss.

FINAL TOUCHES

You can add to the festive look of your home by putting Christmas-themed books (hint: such as this one) and magazines around the house and festive-scented candles to add to the ambiance.

Don't forget to take pictures of everything!

4 THOUGHTFUL GIFTS AND THE TRAP OF GIFT GUIDES

Christmas doesn't come from the store. Maybe Christmas perhaps means a little bit more.

- DR. SEUSS – "The Grinch That Stole Christmas"

The masterfully wrapped presents under the Christmas tree are undoubtedly part of the Christmas magic. With the right approach you can take the stress out of gift shopping and make sure that everybody loves your gifts.

But the art of choosing truly thoughtful gifts that match the personality of the recipient is a different story altogether. There are too many people that actually buy the gifts for themselves, thinking that if they love that item so will the gift recipient. Generally, this couldn't be further from the truth. I know, I know, we are taught that any gift is a perfect gift and that we should be grateful for receiving it in the first place. And of course, we should be gracious and show our appreciation for any gift we receive.

Christmas Tradition

Gifts are exchanged on 6 January in Italy, during the Epiphany, the Three Wise Men are said to have reached Bethlehem bearing gifts for baby Jesus. An old-lady figure who rides a broomstick, called La Befana, brings gifts for well-behaved Italian children.

On the other hand, too many gifts end up as clutter hidden in someone's home. Such gifts are in fact a missed opportunity for actually making someone happy. Not to mention the impact to the environment by adding to the mindless consumerism and waste.

That's why we can take responsibility and take a little time to plan ahead and consider what the gift recipient might actually enjoy receiving. Think of his or her values, likes and dislikes, hobbies and interests. Maybe they mentioned needing or wanting something lately. Usually, just from a short 5 minutes brainstorming session you can come up with a few thoughtful gift ideas that will surely delight the recipient. Next, you can put on your detective hat and check if those ideas are viable by asking questions and snooping around.

If you'd like to read more about choosing better gifts that people will love, check out my book titled <u>"Find That Perfect Gift: Easy Steps to Quickly Find Great Gifts for Any Occasion"</u>, available on

Amazon. It's a short read, and for the price of a coffee it can save you a lot of trouble and even make a few future gift recipients very happy.

To minimize unwanted or ill-chosen gifts, encourage family members or friends to circulate lists or otherwise share what they would like to receive from Santa. Don't be afraid to ask questions and fish for suggestions, people will be more than happy to share their wishes and then maybe reciprocate the whole process.

Should you find yourself in the position to choose a gift for someone that you know little about, just follow a few guidelines:

- make it Christmas themed and maybe even consumable such as a basket of goodies, a bottle of gingerbread gin and other seasonal items

- it shouldn't be anything too large (in case she hates it and on top of that she also has to carry the gift home and then struggle to find a place for the contraption)

- it should be something that (at least in theory) can be easily re-gifted.

RANDOM GIFT GUIDES

Now, let me rant a little bit about the ubiquitous gift guides that you can find all over the Internet. There are even articles titled something like "The Perfect Gift for A Wife". First of all, not all women are the same. Wait, what? Ok, this is in fact common knowledge, but somehow people imagine that all the wives in the world will suddenly like to receive whatever thingamajig it's all the rage on the Internet right now.

This approach is wrong on so many levels. The chance to find a gift that your wife or husband would love to receive from Santa on a random gift guide on the Internet is just as slim as you winning the lottery this week.

"The best of all gifts around any Christmas tree: the presence of a happy family all wrapped up in each other."

-BURTON HILLS

The irony is that people waste far more time browsing random gift guides than just taking 5 to 10 minutes to actually think about their wife or husband and their unique personality.

All these gift guides can be indeed useful, but only after identifying some actually thoughtful gift ideas and further going down the rabbit hole to find the perfect item from that category. Once you narrow it down to say bullet journaling or hiking gear or whatever he or she is really interested in, then you can start browsing the Internet or hit the shops for the actual gift.

GIFT EXPERIENCE

Don't forget that you can gift an experience, especially for that person who has everything or who's just not into more "things". Spa retreats, rock concerts, sky-diving, chocolate making workshops, you name it. Just make sure it fits with their personal interests and it's something they would surely like to experience.

You could also donate a sum of money on their behalf to their favorite charity for instance – should you know that they take a special interest in that area.

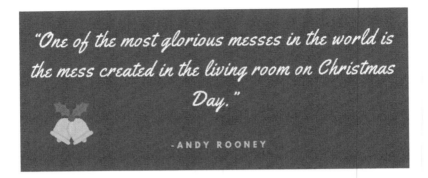

"One of the most glorious messes in the world is the mess created in the living room on Christmas Day."

-ANDY ROONEY

SECRET SANTA AMONG FRIENDS

Consider organizing a Secret Santa amongst friends, colleagues or even family members. Everyone picks a name at random and buys that person a present, anonymously, and within an agreed budget. Everyone will get one really good gift, instead of lots of little ones and it saves time and money. Plus, you can have the fun of trying to guess who your Secret Santa is.

WRAP IT UP

The art of gift giving refers to both offering the gift with grace and to paying attention to the actual packaging. The perfect gift is thoughtful, creative and well-planned. That being said, do not forget about the wrapping.

Get creative with the packaging. Never, ever, underestimate the sheer fun of unwrapping presents. It doesn't have to be tons of wrapping papers and gigantic bow ties – a well-chosen gift bag can do the trick as well. It all depends of course on the recipient's "profile" and little details can go a long way.

Sometimes, quantity can mean quality, when it's a bunch of small individually wrapped items. Guaranteed fun and something to remember and share with friends.

Last but not least, do not forget to include a handwritten card, that is definitely the finishing touch of a thoughtful gift. A few words from the heart, or even just your signature on a well-chosen card printed with a funny message will do the trick.

5 KIDS: ACTIVITIES, BOOKS AND GAMES

At Christmas play and make good cheer,
For Christmas comes but once a year.

- THOMAS TUSSER, English poet and farmer

Even before Christmas, set some time aside during the month of December to do festive activities with the kids. And, don't let anyone know, but you can actually enjoy all the following activities by yourself if you feel crafty this year.

Spend quality time with your children, your nephews and nieces over the festive season doing fun activities together and making memories to cherish.

CHRISTMAS EVE

This is a magical time, the Christmas tree almost turns into a portal to a magical world and it's the best time for stories, watching a classical movie or guessing when will Santa arrive. Of course, some uncle will always see Santa's sleigh out the window and the kids will rush over only to barely miss it. But this sighting will make their night even more magical nevertheless. Hang up the Christmas stockings and dream of sweet gifts.

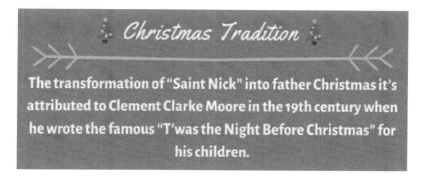

Christmas Tradition

The transformation of "Saint Nick" into father Christmas it's attributed to Clement Clarke Moore in the 19th century when he wrote the famous "T'was the Night Before Christmas" for his children.

On Christmas Eve, before the children got to bed, don't forget to put out some biscuits and a glass of milk for Santa!

CHRISTMAS CARDS

Making your own Christmas cards can be both fun and rewarding, especially when the kids are involved. You can buy card-making packs from craft shops. Pick from a wide array of stamps, stickers, glitter, and special paints. Draw some inspiration from Pinterest and let your creativity run wild.

Look for the Christmas cards received in the previous years - I hope you saved them! They can be used for several craft projects such as Christmas collages, card-making, decorating gift boxes, turning them into gift tags and so on.

HANDMADE CHRISTMAS SOAP

This is a perfumed project: make your own festive soap to give as a gift or to leave out in the guest bathroom.

Place any glycerin-based soap in a sealed, thick plastic bag and simmer in boiling water for up to five minutes until the glycerin melts.

Find some festive-shaped silicon ice-cube molds. Put some dried leaves, flowers or pieces of fruit at the bottom of the molds then cut the corner of the plastic bag and pour the soap into the molds.

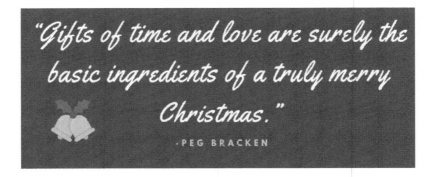

"Gifts of time and love are surely the basic ingredients of a truly merry Christmas."

-PEG BRACKEN

If you feel adventurous, you can create a layered effect by using different colored soaps, to the delight of the kids. Leave to dry completely before removing the soaps from the molds.

CHRISTMAS WREATH

A Christmas wreath is a classic holiday project, you've probably already made quite a few as a child yourself.

A simple version can be made by intertwining fresh fir branches. Or you can use a wire coat hanger pulled out into a circle as a base, to which you can attach small bunches of holly or other evergreen foliage. Bend down the hook to form a loop from which to hang the wreath. Finish off with a few wired pine cones, dried orange slices for a natural look or some Christmas baubles and satin ribbons for a more festive look.

FESTIVE CANDLE HOLDERS

Small terracotta plant pots or small mason jars can be converted into festive candle holders by spraying or painting them gold or silver. Fill them halfway with sand or gravel and put the candle in the center. Add to the base of the candle gold painted pine cones, chestnuts or whatever inspires you.

LETTERS TO SANTA

Make an annual tradition of writing letters to Santa. Use glitter, stickers, paints and crayons and encourage children to decorate their letter in whatever way they like.

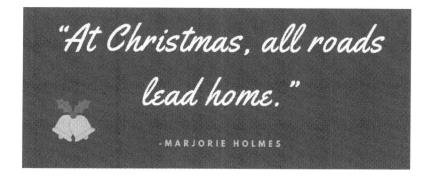

"At Christmas, all roads lead home."

-MARJORIE HOLMES

THE MAD MAHARAJAH PARTY GAME

Kids will love this game, especially those who've just learned how to spell.

In this game, a player stands in the middle of the room, points to another player and says:
'I, the mad maharajah, do not like the letter B (for example). What will you give me to eat?'

The other player must answer with a type of food that does not contain the letter 'B'. Play continues in this way, and with each turn a new letter is announced.

The players must not mention foods containing any of them. And if they do, the mad maharajah is poisoned and dies a very theatrical, epic death. This is obviously the part that the kids really enjoy. The poisoner is out of the game, and another player steps up as maharajah.

THE ABSTRACT POEM GAME

This game will sure stir up some giggles and even some epic laughter episodes.

This is better played with a group of at least 3 friends. The more the merrier. Literally.

You need a long piece of paper and at least one pen. The first player writes the first line of the poem on top of the paper but makes sure to write the last word in that line a bit lower, just below. He or she then folds the paper to cover the line, except for that last word which is written below. Of course, nobody must look and see what the line was about. They will only see the last word.

The next player receives the paper and writes a new line, which must rhyme with that last word. The last word of this new line will also be written below. And so on, until everyone has written at least one verse for a large party or until there is no more paper to write on.

At the end, one of the players will be appointed to be the poet and he will read aloud the masterpiece poem, being as theatrical as he can be. He must force himself not to laugh, which of course will make him laugh even harder.

I used to play this with my cousins as a child and we had tons of fun laughing our faces off.

"Christmas is a piece of one's home that one carries in one's heart."

-FREYA STARK

HOLIDAY BEDTIME

Make bedtime special this time of year by reading festive stories together. Here's a few ideas:

- T'was The Night Before Christmas by Clement Moore – to give you a head start, you can find this glorious classic in the next chapter!

- Father Christmas by Raymond Briggs
- The Father Christmas Letters by J.R.R. Tolkien
- The Lion, the Witch and the Wardrobe, by C.S. Lewis
- The Polar Express by Christ Van Allsburg
- A Christmas Carol by Charles Dickens
- How the Grinch Stole Christmas! By Dr Seuss

6 T'WAS THE NIGHT BEFORE CHRISTMAS

Introduction

Doctor C. Moore wrote this poem for his children. He loved to write poems for them, in fact he even wrote an entire book of poems for his children.

One year he wrote this poem, which we usually call "T'was the Night Before Christmas", to give to his children for a Christmas present.

They read it just after they had hung up their stockings before one of the big fireplaces in their house. Afterward, they learned it, and sometimes recited it, just as other children learn it and recite it *now.*

Now you can read it for your children next to the Christmas tree or with the lights dimmed, just before bedtime.

Twas the Night Before Christmas
A Visit from St. Nicholas
By Clement C. Moore

With Pictures by Jessie Willcox Smith

Houghton Mifflin Company
Boston

T'was the night before Christmas, when all through the house
Not a creature was stirring, not even a mouse;
The stockings were hung by the chimney with care
In hopes that St. Nicholas soon would be there;

The children were nestled all snug in their beds,
While visions of sugar-plums danced in their heads;
And mamma in her kerchief, and I in my cap,
Had just settled our brains for a long winter's nap,

When out on the lawn there arose such a clatter,
I sprang from the bed to see what was the matter.
Away to the window I flew like a flash,
Tore open the shutters and threw up the sash.

The moon on the breast of the new-fallen snow
Gave the lustre of mid-day to objects below,
When, what to my wondering eyes should appear,
But a miniature sleigh, and eight tiny reindeer,

With a little old driver, so lively and quick,
I knew in a moment it must be St. Nick.
More rapid than eagles his coursers they came,
And he whistled, and shouted, and called them by name:

Now, Dasher! now, Dancer! now, Prancer and Vixen!
On, Comet! on, Cupid! on, Donder and Blitzen!
To the top of the porch! to the top of the wall!
Now dash away! dash away! dash away all!"

As dry leaves that before the wild hurricane fly,
When they meet with an obstacle, mount to the sky;
So up to the house-top the coursers they flew,
With the sleigh full of Toys, and St. Nicholas too.

And then, in a twinkling, I heard on the roof
The prancing and pawing of each little hoof.
As I drew in my head, and was turning around,
Down the chimney St. Nicholas came with a bound.

He was dressed all in fur, from his head to his foot,
And his clothes were all tarnished with ashes and soot;
A bundle of Toys he had flung on his back,
And he looked like a peddler just opening his pack.

His eyes—how they twinkled! his dimples how merry!
His cheeks were like roses, his nose like a cherry!
His droll little mouth was drawn up like a bow,
And the beard of his chin was as white as the snow;

The stump of a pipe he held tight in his teeth,
And the smoke it encircled his head like a wreath;
He had a broad face and a little round belly,
That shook when he laughed, like a bowlful of jelly.

He was chubby and plump, a right jolly old elf,
And I laughed when I saw him, in spite of myself;
A wink of his eye and a twist of his head,
Soon gave me to know I had nothing to dread;

He spoke not a word, but went straight to his work,
And filled all the stockings; then turned with a jerk,
And laying his finger aside of his nose,
And giving a nod, up the chimney he rose;

He sprang to his sleigh, to his team gave a whistle,
And away they all flew like the down of a thistle.
But I heard him exclaim, ere he drove out of sight,
"Happy Christmas to all, and to all a good-night."

7 FESTIVE RECIPES, MERRY DRINKS AND GRATITUDE

"Merry Christmas to one and all!"
- Traditional Christmas Dinner Toast

Christmas feasts are the stuff of legends and the times we spend with our families and friends around Christmas dinners are some of the best of our lives.

That being said, this is not the place where you will find elaborate festive recipes as I am not an expert in preparing that type o scrumptious food.

However, if you are in need of some easy recipes that will help you add some tasty bytes to some cozy evenings or to delight a few visitors, this is the right place.

As with everything else, **planning ahead** goes a long way, and here's a few tips:

- Christmas cookie dough can be made and frozen up to a month, then defrosted and used up as needed.

- Most pastry-based treats can also be made ahead of time and frozen.

- Have a few festive cocktail recipes ready just in case some friends drop by.

Christmas Tradition

On 13th of December is Saint's Lucia's Day in Sweden. The oldest daughter of the house is to get up at dawn, dress in a white robe and wear a ring of candles in her hair. She must wake the rest of the family and serve them coffee, buns and cookies.

MENDIANTS

Mendiants are actually chocolate discs with toppings. This is a very easy treat to make and it's great because it can double for a yummy treat around the house for Christmas and a thoughtful handmade gift for your friends or family members. Not to mention that the kids can help with the topping part.

Ingredients:

- chocolate bar of choice – as many as you want; can be white, milk or dark

- dried fruits and any nuts for topping (walnuts, pistachios, and so on).

Preparation method:

Melt the chocolate in a bowl over a saucepan of simmering water. Then spoon onto sheets of parchment paper and add pieces of dried fruits and a variety o nuts on each disc. Don't overdo it.

Leave to cool in the kitchen or place them in the fridge for 1 hour until the chocolate is set. Then gently remove the mendiants from the parchment paper and there you have it: a deliciously simple treat.

ALMOND CHRISTMAS COOKIES

What would Christmas be without some mouthwatering Christmas cookies?

This recipe makes around 40 cookies (plenty to share with friends). If you are more into chocolate chip cookies, you can replace or combine the almonds with chocolate chips.

Ingredients:
8 oz (220 g) softened butter
4 oz (110 g) caster sugar
12 oz (340 g) plain flour, sifted
4 oz (110 g) ground almonds

2 tsp almond essence, optional.

Preparation method:
Preheat the oven to 400°F/200°C.

Cream the softened butter and caster sugar together. Then sing along a happy tune and stir in the flour and ground almonds to form a dough. Now's the time to add the 2 teaspoons of almond essence if desired.

Think merry thoughts and roll the dough out on a dusted surface of choice and cut into festive shapes meant to make Santa's elves jealous. Then place the festive shaped pieces of dough on trays lined with parchment paper.

Bake in the oven for about 8 minutes until pale brown.
Let the cookies cool and enjoy!

Don't forget to always label edible gifts with information about how they should be stored, the date they were made and when they should be eaten by.

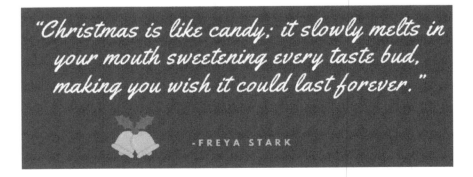

"Christmas is like candy; it slowly melts in your mouth sweetening every taste bud, making you wish it could last forever."

-FREYA STARK

FESTIVE DRINKS

It's time to toast the holiday season with festive fizz, mulled wine and some real Christmas spirit!

TRADITIONAL MULLED WINE

This is a classic and easy to make perfect drink on those cold winter nights.

Ingredients:
1 bottle red wine
1 orange, sliced
4 oz (110 g) sugar – or less
8 cloves
2 cinnamon sticks
a pinch of nutmeg – optional
5 fl oz (150 ml) brandy - optional

Preparation method:

Place all the ingredients in a pot on the stove and simmer gently for about 10 minutes. Reduce heat and stir in the optional brandy. Serve warm in festive looking cups and be merry!

MIMOSA

And now, something for the ladies.

Ingredients:
4.5 fl oz (130 ml) fresh orange juice
1 tsp grenadine
1 bottle of something fizzy such as a Prosecco or Spanish cava.

Preparation method:

Stir together the orange juice and grenadine in a chilled glass. Top up with the fizz and stir again before serving.

EGGNOG

This recipe for the classic and somehow wholesome Christmas drink makes around eight servings.

Ingredients:
the yolks of 12 large eggs
1 lb. (450 g) granulated sugar
45 fl oz (1.3 liter) whole milk
45 fl oz (1.3 liter) spiced rum
1 tsp vanilla extract
45 fl oz (1.3 liter) whipped double cream
pinch of nutmeg

Preparation method:

Start by beating the yolks in a large mixing bowl, then gradually add in the sugar, beating until the mixture thickens. If you are not sure about the consistency of the mixture, quickly look for a video online, it will surely help.

Then stir in the milk, rum and vanilla extract. Gently pour the mixture into a large punch bowl and chill for at least three hours. Fold in the cream just before serving and garnish with the nutmeg and any other finishing touches of choice.

HOT CHOCOLATE

Hot chocolate cannot not be forgotten, as it's the perfect warming beverage for a cozy night in, to sip by the Christmas trees or while watching a holiday movie.

Ingredients:
6 oz (170 g) good-quality dark chocolate
2 fl oz (60 ml) water
18 fl oz (530 ml) milk
2 tablespoons caster sugar
whipped cream
pinch of salt
grated chocolate and/or marshmallows

Preparation method:

In a saucepan melt the chocolate and the water over a low heat. Add a pinch of salt. When the mixture is smooth and glossy, stir in the milk and sugar. Bring to the boil and simmer for about 5 minutes. Gently pour into cups and then top with whipped cream and grated chocolate.

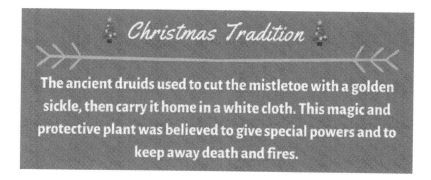

Christmas Tradition

The ancient druids used to cut the mistletoe with a golden sickle, then carry it home in a white cloth. This magic and protective plant was believed to give special powers and to keep away death and fires.

GRATITUDE AND GIVING BACK

Grateful thoughts empower us and make us feel lighter as they open our hearts and ease the tensions of daily life.

Christmas is the perfect time to take a step back and be grateful for all the good things in our lives. Some of them we take for granted and that's why it's a good exercise to sit back and make a list of at least 10 things that you are really grateful for.

You'll see that your list will fill up pretty fast. For instance, I'm grateful for my health, for my wonderful family, for the cozy home we have, for the fact that I got to put this book together and the list goes on and on.

Sure, the nasty, pesky nuisances that happen to us daily can get to us but that's exactly why we must not forget all the goodness we are surrounded by.

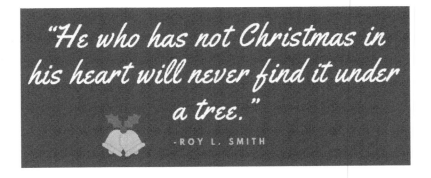

"He who has not Christmas in his heart will never find it under a tree."

-ROY L. SMITH

Here's a short list of ideas of how to **show our gratitude** and give back before the current year is over:

- Most charities produce their own Christmas cards and all of the proceeds go to a good cause

- Some charities organize Christmas Fairs where they sell crafts made by people from shelters, children with special needs and so on. This is a good opportunity to give back and help people in need

- Find charities or NGOs that organize Santa visits to orphanages and prepare a gift for one of the children.

Some of them even send you the letter to Santa of a child so you know exactly what he or she wishes for

- Help others in their activities

- Write Christmas cards to some people that you know would really enjoy to receive holiday greetings

- Write three thank-you emails

- Hug someone special

- Love what you do, do what you love and have a positive attitude.

Don't let the Christmas Craze and general overwhelm get to you. Take a deep breath and remember to **be kind to other people and smile**. People usually smile back, just go ahead and try!

Do not underestimate the power of your general attitude toward things that happen to you. It's your choice to have a good or a bad reaction that will ultimately affect your mood and your actions.

A heart that has been opened by gratitude can choose to approach any predicament with optimism. Faster than any state of mind, gratitude can inspire you to take positive actions and come up with glorious ideas.

Offer hope and encourage other people every time you have the chance to do so. That **positive attitude** and hope are bound to be paid forward in a chain of good deeds.

Don't forget: "The healthiest of all human emotions is gratitude" – Hans Selye.

8 FUN AND GAMES

The business of life is the acquisition of memories.
In the end that's all there is.

- MR. CARSON – Downton Abbey

Playing silly **party games** at home, cozying up on the sofa with a festive-themed **movie**, reading Christmas themed **books** with a big mug of hot cocoa in your hands, there are lots of ways to enjoy the holiday season.

This chapter aims to give you a few jolly ideas and to provide you with some **relaxing activities**. Keep everyone happily occupied this Christmas with games and entertainment for the whole family.

Also, don't forget to get out of the house at least one evening and visit a **traditional Christmas market** to drink mulled wine and browse the little wooden houses for small treasures and festive treats. The Christmas lights and music, the sweets, the roasted chestnuts, the smell of baked apples and cinnamon and the cheerful crowds will all make the trip worth your while.

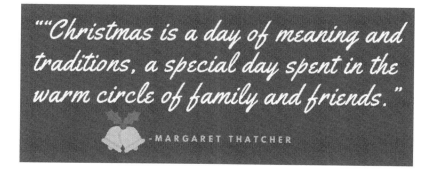

""*Christmas is a day of meaning and traditions, a special day spent in the warm circle of family and friends.*"

-MARGARET THATCHER

Immerse yourself in the Christmas spirit on a festive family day out with something for everyone to enjoy, from ice skating to shopping for holiday reads.

CHRISTMAS MOVIES

There's nothing more festive than cozying up in front of the TV with your loved ones and watching (sometimes for the fifth year in a row) a good Christmas movie.

There are so many to choose from and everybody has got his favorite, but here's a list of the most famous ones:

- It's a Wonderful Life (1946)

- Frosty the Snowman (1969)

- Home Alone – the series
- The Muppet Christmas Carol (1992)
- Scrooged (1988)
- The Nightmare Before Christmas (1993)
- A Christmas Carol (2009)
- Miracle on 34th Street (1994)
- Elf (2003)
- How the Grinch Stole Christmas (2000)
- Love Actually (2003)
- The Holiday (2006)
- National Lampoon's Christmas Vacation (1989)
- Happy Christmas (2016)
- The Santa Clause (1994)
- White Christmas (1954)
- The Bishop's Wife (1948)
- The Man Who Invented Christmas (2017)
- Tokyo Godfathers (2003)
- A Charlie Brown Christmas (1965)
- Arthur Christmas (2011)
- Die Hard (1988)
- The Shop Around the Corner (1940)
- Holiday Inn (1942)

HOSTING A PARTY

If you're hosting a holiday party with friends, here's a few pointers that might make things a bit merrier for everyone:

- get invitations out early as people usually have a few to choose from

- make a playlist in advance

- put together a dress box filled with silly hats and accessories

- if you are serving alcohol make sure you serve food too.

WHO AM I?

An excellent party game for all ages. All you need for this entertaining game is a pen and some paper.

Each player takes a small piece of paper and writes the name of a famous person on it, folds it, and then places it in a hat.

Players take turns to reach into the hat, take out a piece of paper without looking at it and then place it on their forehead for the other players to see. The player will then try to guess their own identity by asking the other players clever questions about the famous person they are supposed to be until they guess who they are.

9 GREEN CHRISTMAS

**Seeing is believing,
but sometimes the most real things in the
world
are the things we can't see.**

- THE POLAR EXPRESS

We all know the importance of sustainability and taking care of the environment. This chapter includes a few easy tips to make sure your Christmas carbon footprint stays small.

Recycle items you have around the house to make beautiful home-made gifts. You can browse Pinterest for different DIY gift ideas.

Do not be afraid to **re-gift**. Where's the good in keeping items that do not fit you or you do not use nor like? Just follow Marie Kondo's advice and if there's something that does not bring you joy try to figure out if you know someone who might truly enjoy receiving that object as a gift.

Buy gifts that are locally made. Many items on sale at Christmas are made cheaply abroad and their transportation contributes significantly to greenhouse emissions. Look for local shops and designers and **support the local economy**.

You can find lots of great gifts made from **recycled materials and fabrics** these days. Try to support these businesses to help reduce the waste stream and support the concept of recycling.

Avoid buying battery-powered gifts and toys. Almost half of all battery sales are made during the holiday season and discarded batteries become an environmental hazard.

Even rechargeable batteries eventually have to be thrown away. Either way, just don't forget to always recycle your used batteries – do not just throw them in the bin. Most supermarkets have a battery drop-off and places like IKEA even gift new batteries in exchange for used ones.

Do not throw away unwanted gifts! As I mentioned before, **re-gift** them to someone else by taking the time to figure out who would really enjoy each item. If there's no match, you can always donate them to some local charities.

Go for quality solar LED light for the outdoor decorations, or at least for some of them.

To save energy, turn off your Christmas tree lights and outdoor lights when going to bed or leave the house. This is also a safety precaution.

I've witnessed these past years several quarrels related to the question: which is the most environmentally friendly – **an artificial tree or a real tree?** Well, I did my research and the conclusion is this: the real tree if it's bought from a sustainable, local source.

And this is why: although an **artificial tree** is reusable from year to year, eventually when it is worn out it will have to be thrown away and will end up in a landfill. Because of their plastic content, these trees are not biodegradable.

You can do your bit for the environment by buying a **real tree** from a sustainable source, where trees are purposely planted and grown for Christmas. Most of these businesses give you the option to return the tree after Christmas and some of them even offer an incentive. These trees will be taken to a wood chipper and the chips will be then used as mulch for the garden for instance.

Some smaller Christmas trees can be bought in a pot and then planted into your garden.

Another way to support a green Christmas is to gift **experiences** instead of buying gifts. Of course, you'll still have to consider the recipient values, hobbies and preferences. You can think of cinema tickets, concert or theater tickets, massage and spa sessions, cooking or craft workshops and so on.

Wrapping paper accounts for huge wastage during the Christmas period, but you can find creative ways to wrap your presents perfectly and also avoid waste. **Reuse gift bags** from presents you received the previous years (never throw these away). You can reuse spare things from your house for wrapping paper, such as: pages from comics, old maps and posters or leftover fabric.

You can buy recycled wrapping paper and personalize it by using paints or old Christmas cards.

Avoid shiny foil paper as this type of material cannot be recycled.

Some other actions that can really make a difference are:

- buy large bottles of drinks instead of multi-packs of small ones to save on packaging

- buy locally produced, organic meat and vegetables to help reduce the impact of transport fuel consumption

- carry your groceries home in reusable fabric bags

- avoid using paper or plastic plates and cups if you are entertaining

- turn down the thermostat by just 2°F/1°C and you will save on energy, carbon emissions and money. Make that 4°F/2°C and it will also be a great excuse to wear your favorite festive reindeer sweater

- avoid buying artificial Christmas decorations each year. Spice things up by using natural materials such as holly, spruce and ivy and keep your current artificial decorations for as long as possible.

10 SECRET SANTA AT THE OFFICE

We have to remember what's important in life: friends, waffles and work.

-    LESLIE KNOPE, Parks and Recreation

Aaah! That time of the year! Secret Santa at the workplace. The time when you have to buy a gift for someone at the office, you have no idea who that person is and you are terrified that yours will be the blandest gift of them all. The one that gets a disappointed look, quickly covered by a fake smile. That gift that no one claims ownership upon, while other colleagues exchange meaningful looks with the very happy recipients of well-conceived, hilarious, cute or witty gifts. Oh, the horror!

Christmas gifts for coworkers can be generally daunting, let alone when the recipient's identity is unknown – leaving the very idea of a personalized gift to be untouchable.

The problem is that people tend to overcomplicate things and think too much into it. This is a matter of less is more and the secret is to **keep it simple**. Gift ideas for coworkers do not have to be that hard to come up with.

Here's a list of some bulletproof gift ideas for Secret Santa at the office:

- a box of assorted chocolates or macaroons, a Christmas themed porcelain mug (it will go straight to the wife if the recipient happens to be a man)

- a "World Domination Plans" notebook

- a bottle of ginger wine

- a set of Christmas themed, colorful or funny socks in a gift box.

Heck, if you know your way around the kitchen you could even bake a batch of cookies and put them in a mason jar. Who doesn't love cookies?

Some other great Secret Santa gift ideas for coworkers are the ones that are sort of "one size fits all", something that would work for pretty much anyone, regardless of sex, age or personality type:

- a paperback Christmas Planner/Organizer

- a cozy Christmas themed book

- a box of fancy herbal tea blend with holiday spices such as orange, cinnamon, baked apples, cloves or nutmeg

- an extravagant winter holidays scented candle

- high quality Christmas tree decorations, maybe from an upmarket well-known brand

Just pick something along those lines that is most convenient for you to buy, bake or order. You don't have to drive to the other side of town or make a huge fuss about it. Make sure you have it ready and nicely wrapped on time.

Generally, a good Secret Santa gift is something that can be easily regifted (at least in theory). In addition, don't trust the endless random gift guides on the Internet that try to sell you all sorts of useless objects that will only end up as clutter in someone's closet. If it doesn't have a Christmassy vibe, it's not a good fit.

Do not underestimate **the power of gift wrapping** for this particular occasion. As the gift is small or in any case it had to fit within a given budget, the wrapping can go a long way. This is the place to splurge, go wild, use a huge bow, glitter, fancy gift bags and whatever else inspires you.

If you really want your Secret Santa gift to be the star of the day, just frame a large photo of your team's manager, or even the company CEO, wrap it nicely and there you have it. Just make sure to use only official photos from the company's internal files and perhaps let the manager know about your plot. This cool Christmas gift for your coworker will be remembered for years and years to come until it finally becomes the stuff of legend around the office. Mwell, I might be exaggerating a bit but seriously, people will be talking about this for weeks.

I know a guy who received a framed photograph of one of his colleagues who was temporarily mentoring him for a project. In this case the identity of the receiver was known and the identity of the one offering the gift was secret. The idea of having a framed photo of his peer coworker on his office desk was hilarious and everyone had fun for days. The gift that keeps giving.

Another aspect to consider is the agreed budget. Do not think that by exceeding this budget you're doing a good deed. The other colleagues that did stick to the agreed budget might feel somehow cheated, because they made an effort to find something cute and thoughtful within that budget.

The point is, keep it Christmas themed or slightly funny, choose something small but high quality rather than a big shady contraption on sale, stick to the agreed budget and you'll be just fine.

11 FESTIVE CARTOONS, JOKES AND DRAWINGS

The best way to spread Christmas cheer is singing loud for all to hear.

- BUDDY THE ELF

Relax, eat, drink and be merry! Oh, and have e few laughs and giggles.

HO-HO-HO CHRISTMAS JOKES

Q: What kind of Christmas music do elves like?
A: "Wrap" music

Q: How can Santa deliver presents during a thunderstorm?
A: His sleigh is flown by "raindeer"

Q: How to you know Santa knows karate?
A: He has a black belt.

Q. Why do Dasher and Dancer love coffee?
A. Because they're Santa's star bucks!

Q: What do you call people who are afraid of Santa Claus?
A: Claustrophobic.

Q: How is Christmas just like your job?
A: You do all the work and the fat guy in the suit gets all the credit.

Q: How did the ornament get addicted to Christmas?
A: He was hooked on tree his whole life.

Q: What Christmas Carol do parents like best?
A: Silent Night.

Q: What did one snowman say to the other snowman?
A: Can you smell carrot?

Grab some pencils and color your way into a wonderful Christmas!

THE END

MERRY CHRISTMAS!

ABOUT THE AUTHOR AND BONUS LINKS

Lia Manea is the author of _Find That Perfect Gift! Easy Steps to Find Great Gifts for Any Occasion_, Amazon Bestseller, a how to book on choosing truly thoughtful gifts that people will love. It has been described as a road map to figuring out how make your loved ones happy for their birthday or other occasions. Find out how to show your wife or husband that you care and maybe how to totally impress your mother in law. Make sure to check out her **coloring books** as well!

She left the finance corporate world a few years back, so she could better take care of her family, follow her interests and continue to learn and grow.

She is currently an author, interior decorator, happy mother of one and part of a beautiful family. It may come as no surprise, but she loves reading books, watching movies and making sure that nothing goes to waste. She occasionally travels the world, as her explorer instincts kick in several time a year (much to the dismay of her husband).

If you enjoyed this little book, **please leave a review** on Amazon- just click the "Write a customer review" button on the book page. Even a line or two would be incredibly helpful! Reviews are what make other readers consider picking up this book and decide whether it is a good fit for their needs. Don't forget click Follow under my picture so you find out about new book releases.

Don't forget to download your **Christmas Planner Printables** here: https://storyoriginapp.com/giveaways/688e1c24-c90e-11ea-aed1-cb3f13679c84. All you have to do is print them each year and use the templates over and over again.

Or drop me a line at lia.manea.perfectgift@gmail.com and I'll email you the link. Enjoy!

LAST BUT NOT LEAST: A BONUS

As a small gift for my readers, I've put together a Checklist for Great Gifts and 3 Common Mistakes to Avoid – go ahead and download it here: https://findthatperfectgift.weebly.com/your-checklist.html

And while you're there, join my lively email list where I rant about gifts, holidays and I share book promos from fellow authors.

Finally, please feel free to follow my page on Facebook @PerfectGiftGuide for the occasional gift tips and tricks and stellar memes.

Thank you for reading!